Dot-to-Dot
FAMOUS PAINTINGS

Dot-to-Dot

FAMOUS PAINTINGS

Join the dots to discover the world's best-loved masterpieces

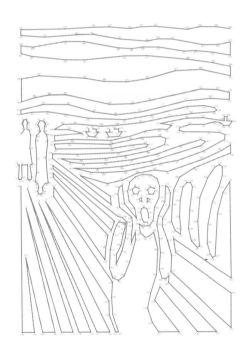

Jeni Child

southwater

Introduction

Dot-to-dot puzzles have long been a popular activity for young and old alike, with the opportunity to happily while away the hours uncovering hidden paintings, animals, buildings and places. This fabulous new book takes simple join-the-dot art to the next level with 40 puzzles of famous paintings to complete. Intricate, challenging and rewarding to finish, the puzzles range from 250 to 1060 dots and will have you transfixed as you progress from dot to dot trying to see what image materializes.

An absorbing and relaxing activity that can calm and reduce daily stresses and anxieties, these brain-stimulating puzzles can contribute to alertness. There are also proven educational benefits to doing dot-to-dot activities. It helps to build fine motor skills, improve concentration levels and strengthen mapping skills – all while creating memorable art to enjoy. Each drawing may take approximately half an hour to complete, perfect for a rainy day or holiday activity, or simply a chance to take yourself away for some peace and quiet for a while.

The famous masterpieces featured here are best-loved paintings from world-class masters, including self-portraits, landscapes, theatre scenes, still-life compositions and contemporary abstract art. They are all outstanding examples that represent the history of fine-art painting and have been studied and argued over many times by art critics.

These wonderful paintings have been captured as dot-to-dot puzzles, their identities waiting patiently to emerge from the depth of the dots to reveal who they are.

As some of the drawings are quite intricate in parts it is best to use a pen (rather than a pencil) with a fine tip. Starting at number 1, connect the dots in numerical order. If a number is next to a circle rather than a dot, lift your pen and start again at the next consecutive number. This number may not necessarily be close to the previous number, it can be anywhere on the design.

Continue completing the picture in this manner, picking up your pen whenever you come to a circle until you have come to the last dot. For the most accurate picture, try to keep a relatively straight line between the connecting dots, but don't worry if you make a mistake or have a wobbly line, it won't affect the finished piece.

Once you have completed your dot-to-dot artwork, turn to the back of the book where you can compare your work with the finished solution and also read some interesting facts about the painting you have drawn.

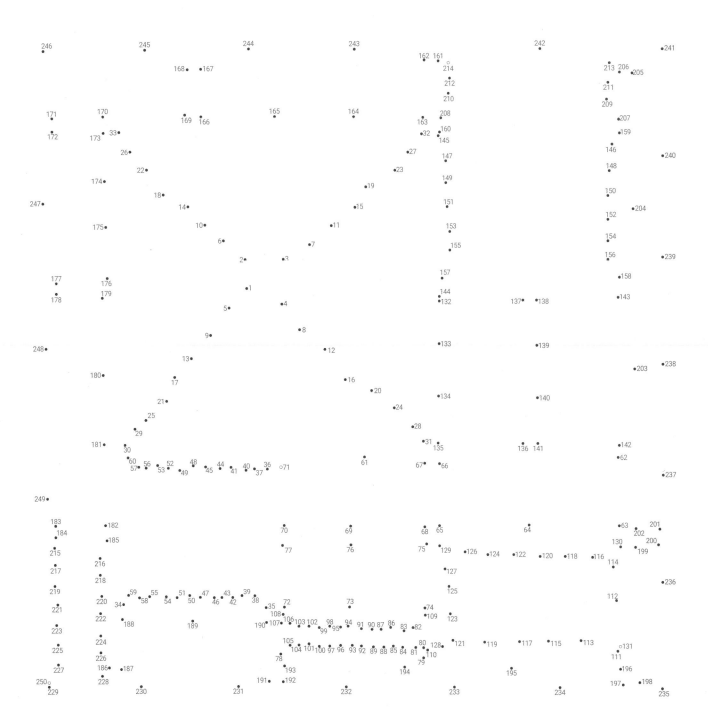

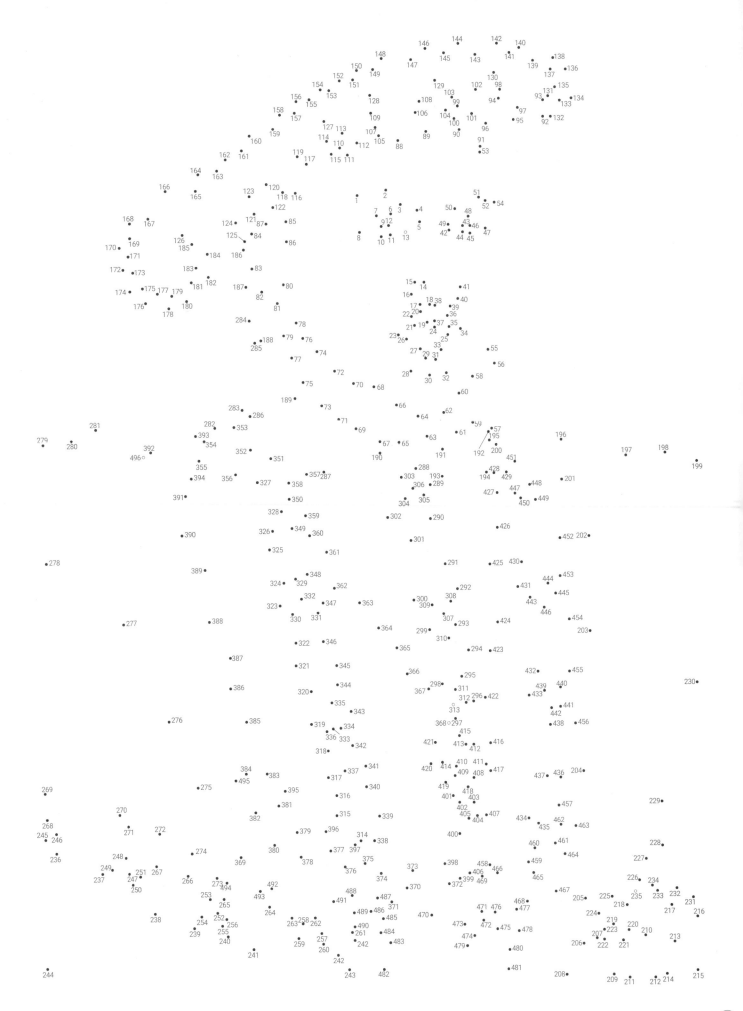

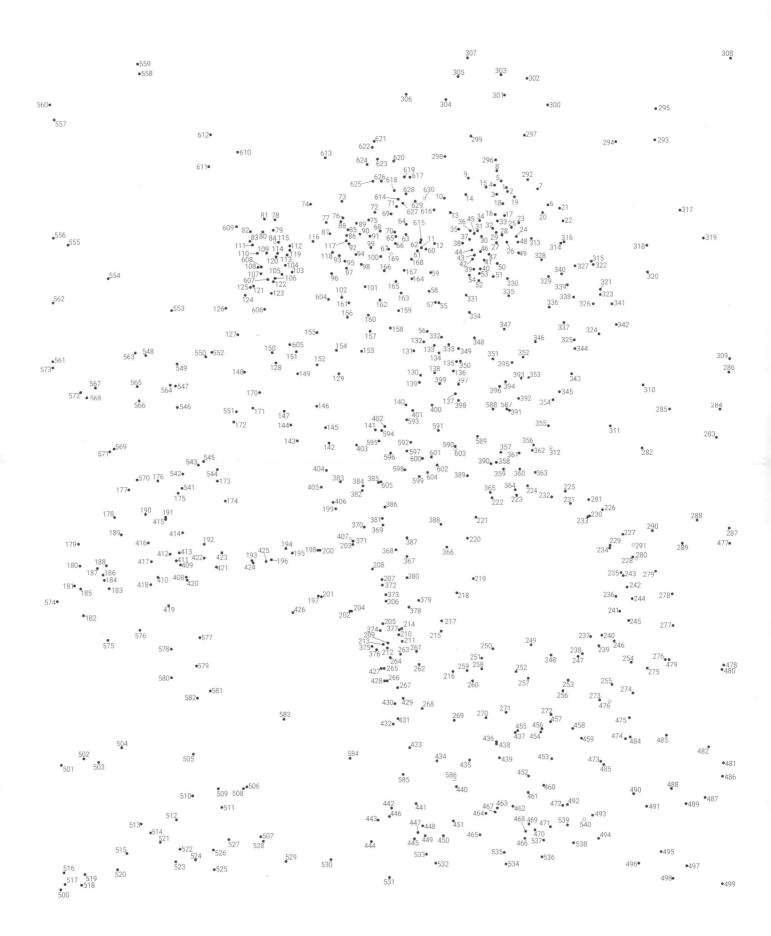

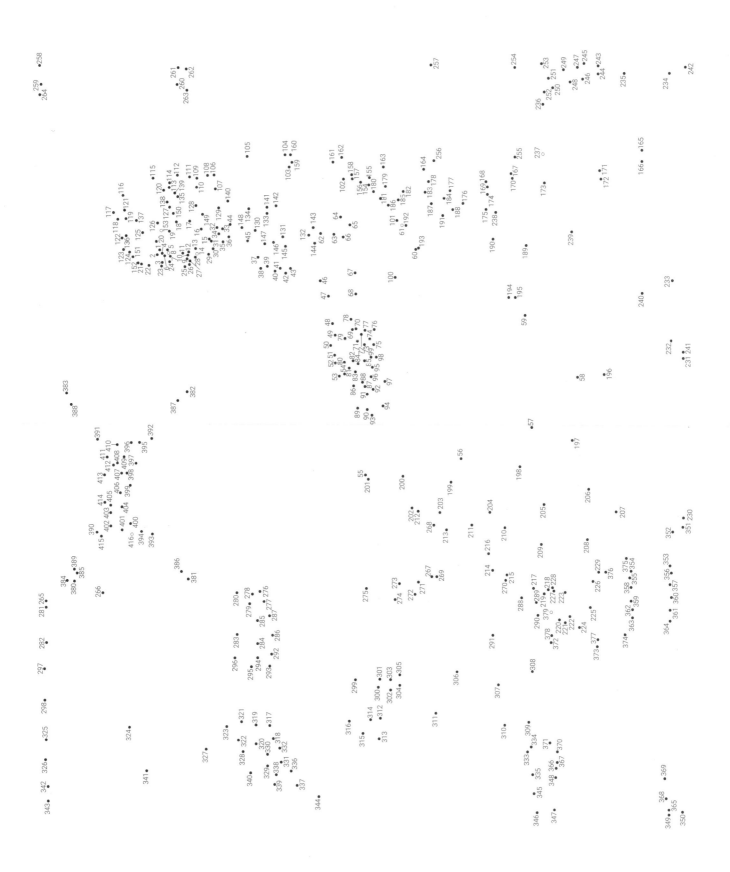

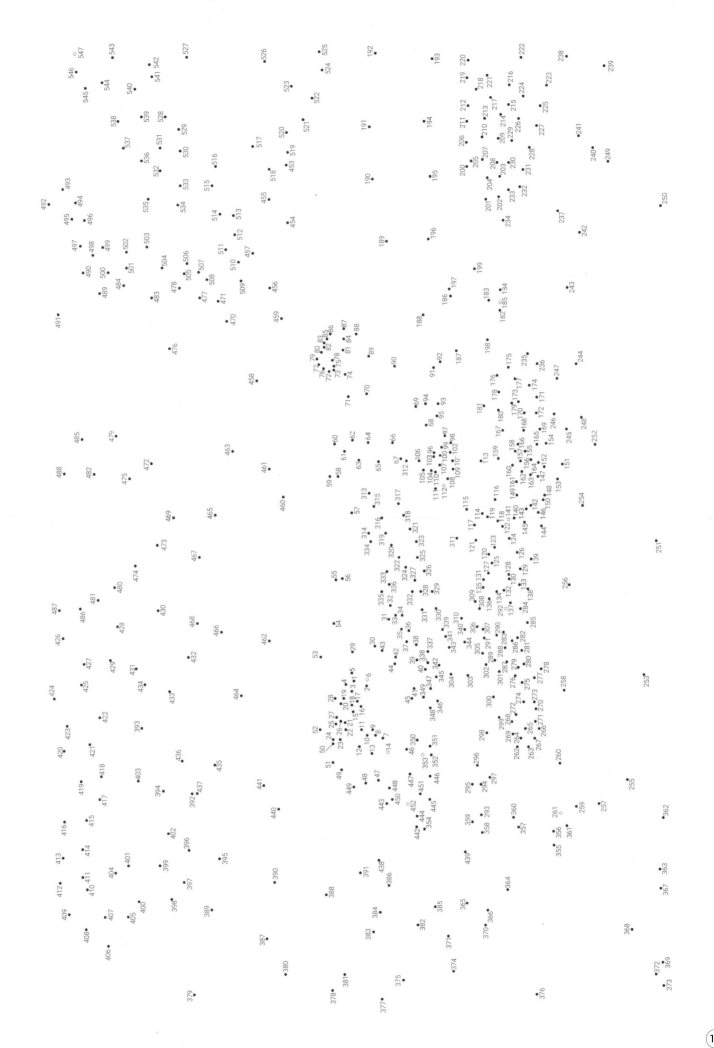

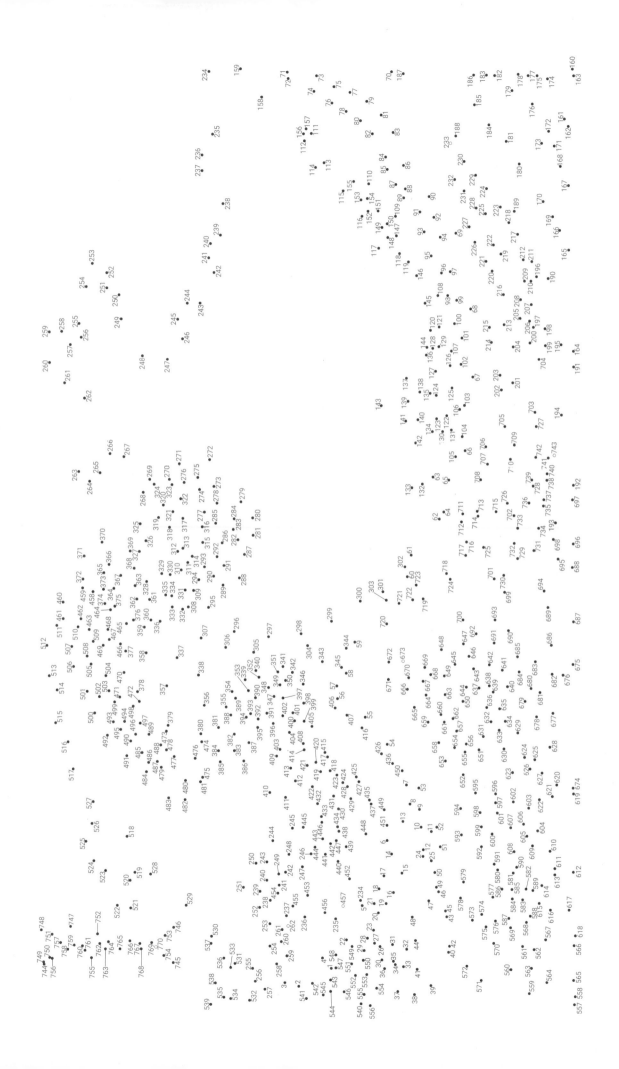

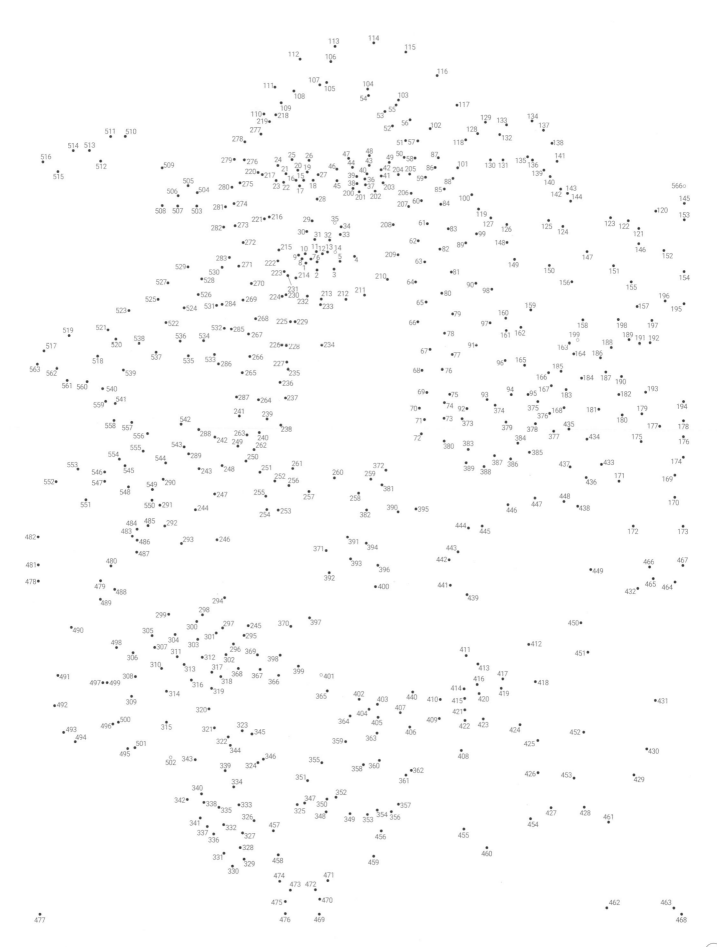

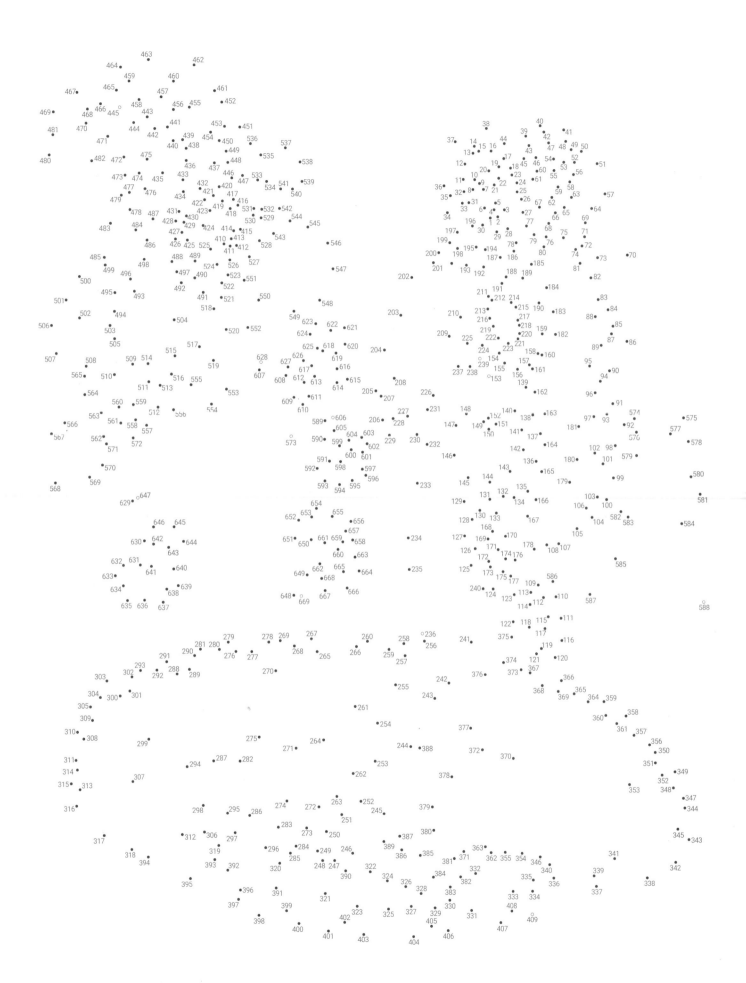

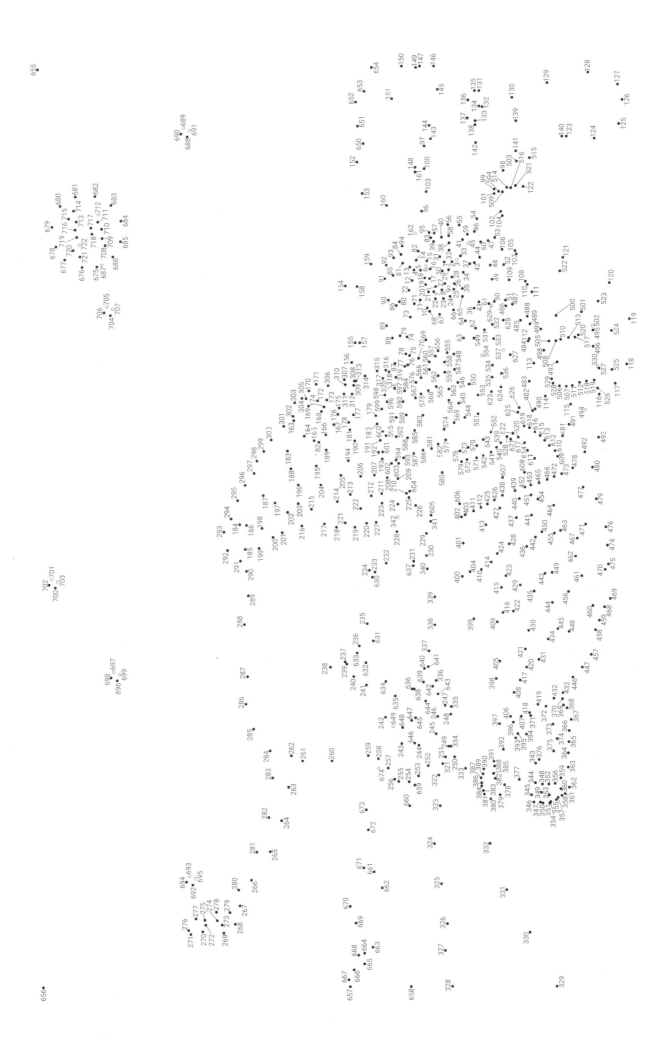

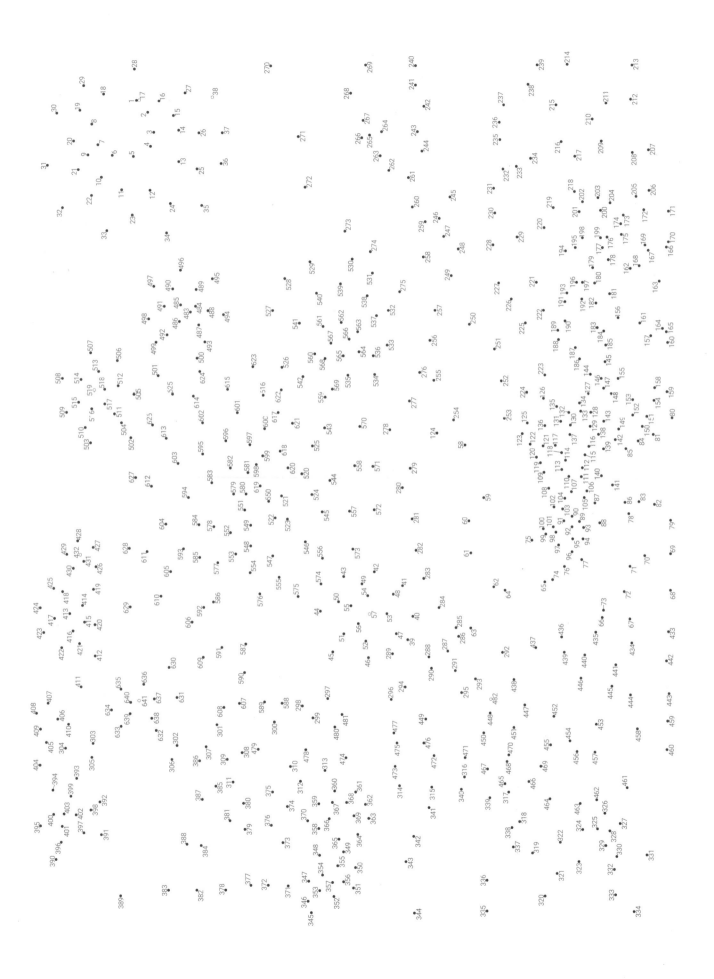

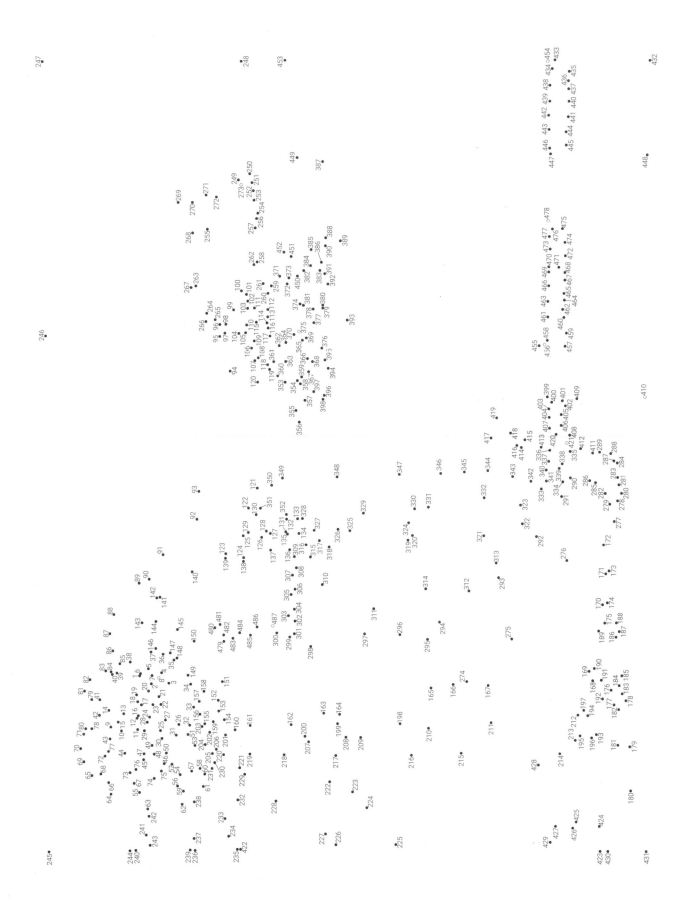

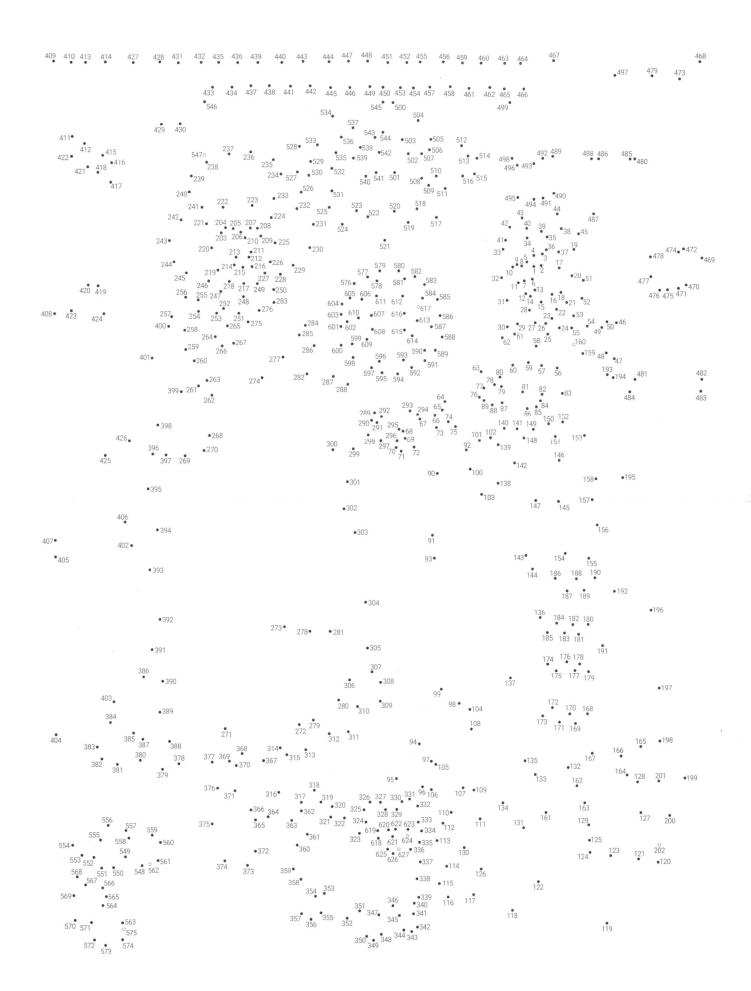

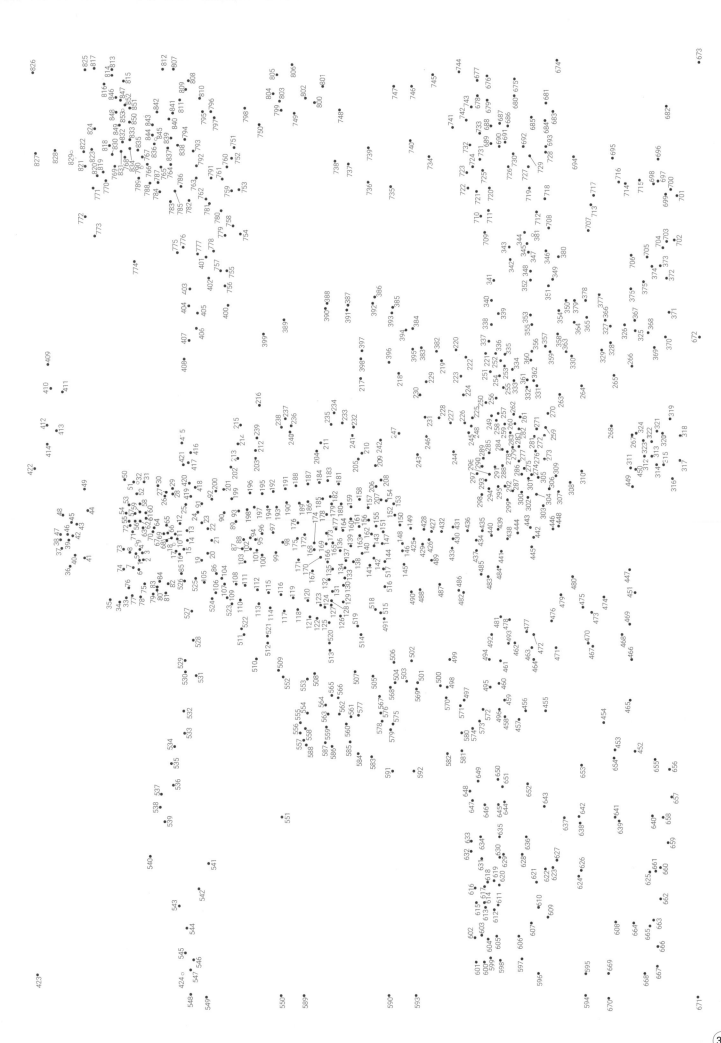

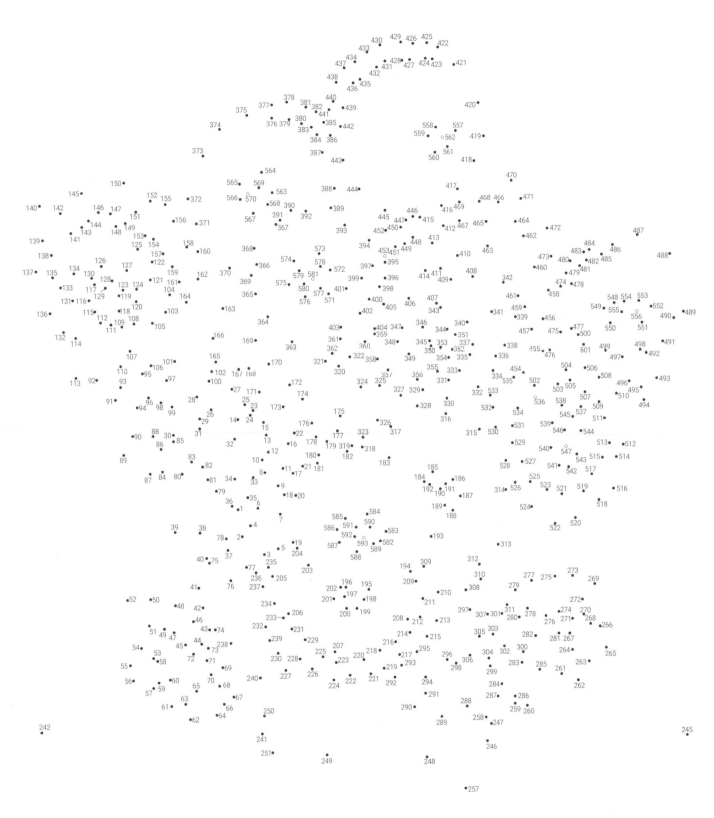

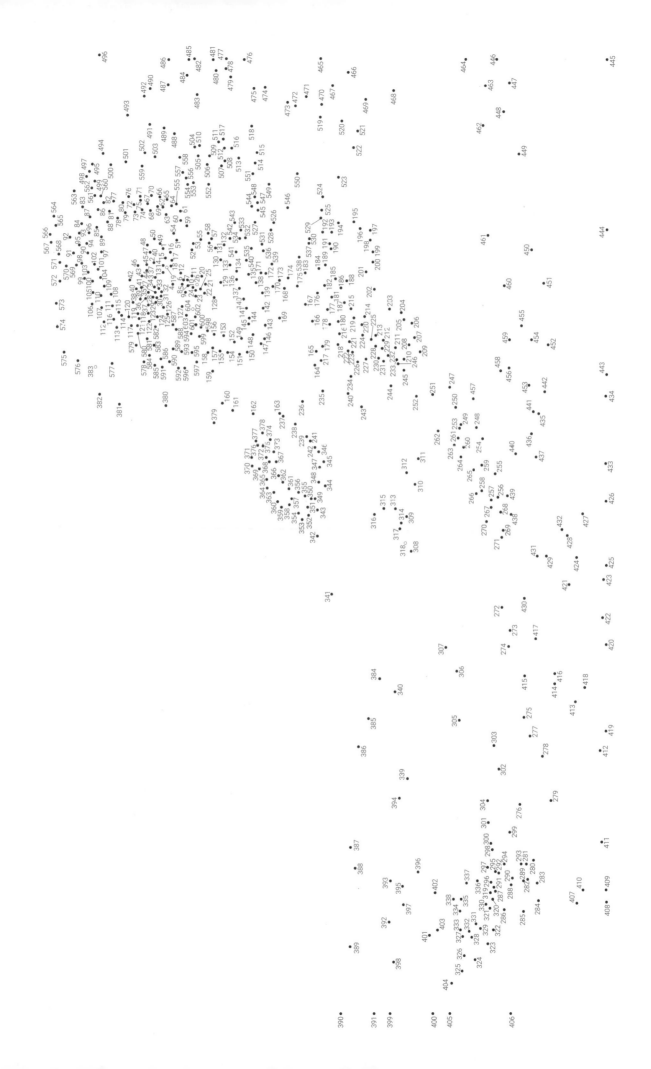

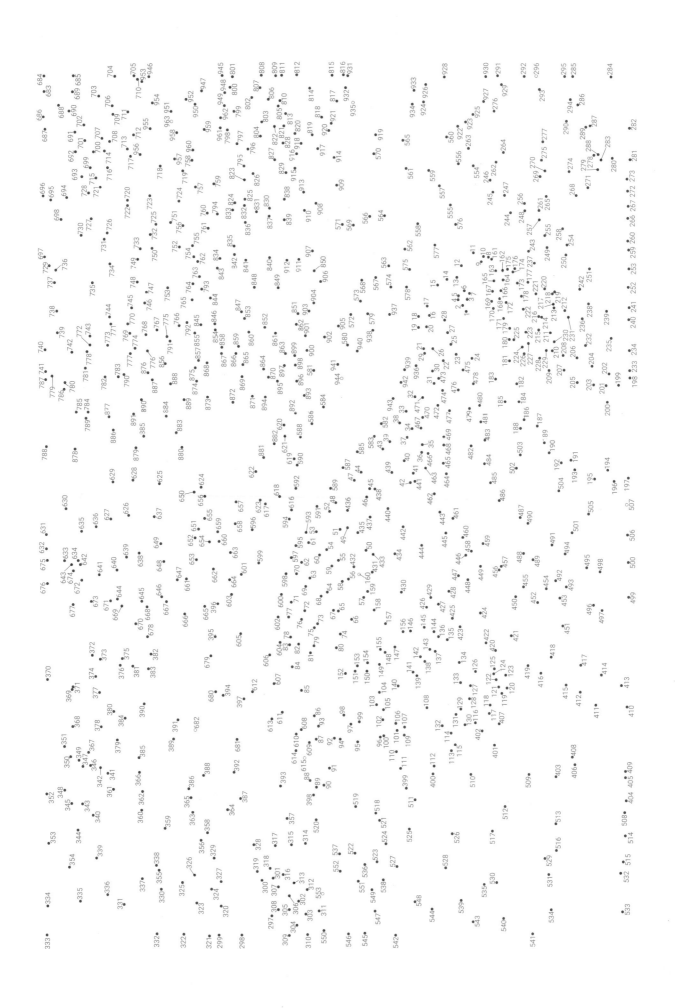

Page 1

Blue Nude II, 1952 by Henri Matisse
(1869–1954)

Matisse was one of the most influential painters and sculptors of the 20th century, and his series of cut outs, 'Blue Nudes', is of particular note. All four nudes feature a reclined woman with intertwined legs and an arm stretched behind her back, based on the relaxed woman from his earlier painting 'Le Bonheur de Vivre'. **250 dots**

Page 2

Girl with a Pearl Earring, c. 1665 by Johannes Vermeer
(1632–1675)

The phrase 'Girl with a Pearl Earring' is perhaps most famous today for the 2003 film starring Scarlett Johannson, but it is also the name of the painting that inspired the film. Mysteries remain about the identity of the girl, what she was thinking and her relationship with Vermeer, and these unanswerable questions are a part of the work's popularity. **300 dots**

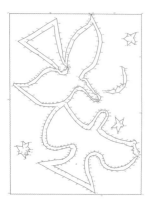

Page 3

Les Deux Oiseaux, 1953 by Georges Braque
(1882–1963)

The distinctive painting 'Les Deux Oiseaux' or 'The Two Birds', is held in the Louvre Museum in Paris, decorating the ceiling of the Henry II hall. Braques was 70 years old when he was commissioned by Georges Salles, director of the Museums of France, to produce the work. 'Les Deux Oiseaux' is inspired by the flight of flamingos that Braques saw in a bird reserve. **445 dots**

Page 4

The Son of Man, 1946 by René Magritte
(1898–1967)

This surrealist painting is in fact a self-portrait, with Magritte's eyes peeking out behind the apple. Magritte enjoyed juxtaposing ordinary elements in unusual ways, and the motifs of apples and bowler hats reappeared in many of his works. Magritte said of this painting, "Everything we see hides another thing, we always want to see what is hidden by what we see." **252 dots**

Page 5

Still Life with Skull, 1898 by Paul Cézanne (1839–1906)

This is one of the most prominent paintings of the vanitas style, an artistic genre concerned with the meaninglessness of earthly life and the transient nature of all earthly pursuits. Cézanne's works grew darker as he advanced in age: the mix of fresh and rotting fruit in this painting was displaced by an increasing number of skulls, culminating in 'Pyramid of Skulls' (c.1901). **523 dots**

Page 6

Woman with a Flower, 1891 by Paul Gauguin (1848–1903)

Gauguin travelled to Tahiti in 1891 and drew several paintings of Tahitians, including 'Woman with a Flower', one of the very first pictures he painted on the island. Gauguin described his sitter's mouth as having been "modelled by a sculptor who knew how to put into a single mobile line a mingling of all joy and all suffering." **606 dots**

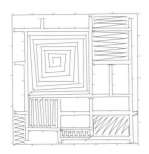

Page 7

Composition with Large Red Plane, Yellow, Black, Grey, and Blue, 1921 by Piet Mondrian (1872–1944)

This is the most famous of Dutch artist Mondrian's Neo-Plasticism works, a non-representational form consisting of a white ground with a grid of black lines and the three primary hues on top. Although a popular form of modern art now, at the time it was unusual to paint in such a minimalist, block-patterned style. **250 dots**

Page 8

Whistlejacket, c. 1762 by George Stubbs (1724–1806)

The star racehorse Whistlejacket was owned by the Marquess of Rockingham who invited Stubbs to Wentworth House, his country house in Yorkshire. Stubbs was a specialist equine artist and this portrait of an animal is in a style usually reserved for supreme human figures. The painting stands at almost three metres (ten feet) high, with nothing to focus on apart from the regal horse. **342 dots**

Page 9

Portrait of Henry VIII, 1537 by Hans Holbein the Younger (1497–1543)

Hans Holbein's work has become the defining image of Henry VIII. Originally created as part of a mural showing the Tudor dynasty at the Palace of Whitehall, it was destroyed by fire in 1698 but lives through its many copies that were made on Henry's command and distributed around the realm. It has been described as a piece of propaganda for the way it enhances Henry's power and majesty. **496 dots**

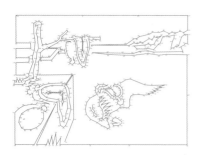

Page 10

The Persistence of Memory, 1931 by Salvador Dali (1904–1989)

Commonly referred to as 'The Melting Watches,' this surrealist painting is Dali's most well-known work. He would enter states of self-induced psychotic hallucinations when painting it, often surprising and terrifying himself at what he had produced when he woke up. Dali credits the inspiration for this painting as a wheel of Camembert cheese that had melted in the sun. **513 dots**

Page 11

Napoleon Crossing the Alps, 1801 by Jacques-Louis David (1748–1825)

French artist David had a tumultuous relationship with Napoleon, and had several arguments with the French leader about this series of five paintings. Bonaparte was less interested in being physically represented accurately and more keen on having his greatness displayed for propaganda purposes. The painting became an idealised depiction of the real crossing Napoleon and his army made through the Alps at the Great St. Bernard Pass in 1800. **632 dots**

Page 12

Self Portrait with Two Circles, c. 1660 by Rembrandt (1606–1669)

Rembrandt painted more than 40 self-portraits in his career, but this one stands out for its honesty in his aged appearance, complete with eyebrow grooves and drooping jowls. The hand-on-hip stance and intense stare give a confrontational appearance, implying a master solemnly asserting his genius. The work is considered one of the greatest paintings of his later years. **408 dots**

Page 13

Jacqueline with Flowers, 1954 by Pablo Picasso (1881–1973)

Picasso met 27-year-old Jacqueline Roque when he was 72 and they married two years later when his first wife Olga Koklova died. 'Jacqueline with Flowers' is an example of Picasso's abstract cubism. With her long neck, high cheekbones and regal posture, Jacqueline has been described as 'the modern sphinx', and she continued to be the subject of Picasso's paintings until his death. **547 dots**

Page 14

An Angel Playing a Flageolet, c. 1878 by Edward Burne-Jones (1833–1898)

Burne-Jones painted several angels playing instruments throughout his career, but he felt particularly attached to this painting, keeping it in his studio for ten years before releasing it to be sold. It is painted in tempera, a medium that involved the mixing of pigments with water and egg yolk, a popular style in the Renaissance but very uncommon in the late 19th century. **589 dots**

Page 15

American Gothic, 1930 by Grant Wood (1891–1942)

This is one of the most parodied paintings in the history of art. Wood used his sister and dentist to pose as "the kind of people I fancied should live in that house". He had discovered the little white cottage while visiting Iowa and made sketches of it at the time, adding the figures when he was back in his studio. Local Iowans resented the dour portrayal of the couple to the world. **485 dots**

Page 16

Symphony in Grey and Black, No. 1: Portrait of the Artist's Mother, 1871 by James Abbott McNeill Whistler (1834–1903)

Popularly known as 'Whistler's Mother' this painting captures a somewhat solemn Anna McNeill Whistler posing for her son. Contemporary reviews focused on the spare and unflattering portrayal of the painter's mother whilst Whistler insisted that the sitter's identity was secondary to the painting's aesthetic purpose of organizing shape and hue in a pleasing manner. **416 dots**

Page 17

Self-Portrait with Bandaged Ear, 1889 by Vincent van Gogh (1853–1890)

The later years of van Gogh's life were plagued with mental health problems and episodes of self-destruction. The most famous of these was when he severed off part of his ear with a razor after a confrontation with the artist Paul Gauguin. This self-portrait was painted after he was released from hospital and depicts the artist in a still and melancholic mood. **498 dots**

Page 18

Ophelia, 1852 by John Everett Millais (1829–1896)

The tragic, poetic death scene of Ophelia in Shakespeare's 'Hamlet' inspired Millais's painting, depicting the character singing in a river before she drowns. The painter persuaded his 19-year-old muse Elizabeth Siddall (later changed to Siddal) to pose in a cold bathtub fully clothed for hours at a time, which resulted in illness. 'Ophelia' has been held in the Tate Britain for over a century. **547 dots**

Page 19

The Great Wave off Kanagawa, c. 1831 by Katsushika Hokusai (1760–1849)

This woodblock print, published between 1830 and 1833, has become an iconic image of the power of the ocean and has even found its way onto mobile phones in the shape of the wave emoji. Sometimes assumed to be a tsunami, it is more likely to be a rogue wave, partially concealing Mount Fuji, the highest peak in Japan. Indeed, 'The Great Wave' is the most famous of Hokusai's series 'Thirty-six Views of Mount Fuji'. **770 dots**

Page 20

Le Grand Canal, Venice, 1908 by Claude Monet (1840–1926)

Monet had described Venice as "too beautiful to paint" before he undertook this series of 37 paintings at the peak of his career. 'Le Grand Canal' depicts the Baroque church of Santa Maria della Salute, but unlike many paintings of Venice it is less concerned with representing famous monuments and more interested in the play of light and reflection on the water. **475 dots**

Page 21

Mona Lisa, c. 1506 by Leonardo da Vinci (1452–1519)

Undoubtedly the most famous painting in the world, the 'Mona Lisa' has been visited, written about and parodied more than any other art work. Thought to be a painting of Lisa Gherardini, the wife of Francesco del Giocondo, the model's enigmatic half-smile alone has produced centuries of discussion. The Italian name for the painting, 'La Gioconda', means jocund (happy or jovial), and is a pun on Lisa's married name Giocondo. **566 dots**

Page 22

Dancer with a Bouquet of Flowers, 1878 by Edgar Degas (1834–1917)

Degas is considered one of the founders of Impressionism (although it was a term he despised, preferring to call his works 'realist'), and more than half his works depict dancers. Despite the joy and movement in paintings such as 'Dancer with a Bouquet of Flowers', Degas himself was reported to be a misanthropic, anti-Semitic loner who alienated most of his friends. **474 dots**

Page 23

The Scream, 1893 by Edvard Munch (1863–1944)

This famous image has been parodied in everything from 'Dr Who' to 'The Simpsons'. Part of a series of four, 'The Scream' was created at a low point in Munch's life, when he was penniless, heartbroken and worried about developing a family mental illness. The bridge was a popular spot for suicide jumpers and was in earshot of a lunatic asylum where Munch's schizophrenic sister resided. **436 dots**

Page 24

The Card Players, 1882-95 by Paul Cézanne (1839–1906)

Not one painting but a series of five, 'The Card Players' is an example of Cézanne bridging the gap between 19th-century Impressionism and 20th-century Cubism. The first of the five paintings featured five card players, which Cézanne reduced to four for the second painting. For the final three paintings, there are only two players featured, bringing the painting into a symmetrical balance. **582 dots**

Page 25

The Birth of Venus, c. 1486 by Sandro Botticelli (c. 1446–1510)

One of the most famous and appreciated works of art, 'The Birth of Venus' has sparked debate for centuries about its meaning and allegorical references. The image of the goddess Venus emerging from the sea in an open shell has become a lasting symbol of divine beauty. The painting is also credited as the first work on canvas in Tuscany, Italy. **669 dots**

Page 26

Moulin Rouge: La Goulue, 1891 by Henri de Toulouse-Lautrec (1864–1901)

The cabaret Moulin Rouge opened in 1889 and became instantly loved for its risqué performances (with the police making routine checks that the dancers were wearing underwear). French artist de Toulouse-Lautrec produced this work as a poster advertising the club. The silhouetted crowd allows the spotlight to turn on the star performers of the dance floor. **477 dots**

Page 27

The Theatre Box, 1874 by Pierre-Auguste Renoir (1841–1919)

Renoir learnt his trade by studying at the Louvre, and by the 1870s he was a prominent figure in the Impressionist movement. The painting's depiction of an elegant couple in a loge, or theatre box, is considered a masterpiece of Impressionism and exemplifies the movement's interest in the spectacle of modern life, where the audience is of as much interest as the performers. **624 dots**

Page 28

The Sleeping Gypsy, 1897 by Henri Rousseau (1844–1910)

Rousseau imagined the scenario in this painting: a wandering African gypsy overcome by fatigue falls into a deep sleep and a passing lion picks up her scent but doesn't devour her. The hard lines and flat perspectives were criticized as childlike at the time, but Rousseau has since become recognized as an influential avantgarde artist, despite having no formal training. **722 dots**

Page 29

Starry Night, 1889 by Vincent van Gogh
(1853–1890)

One of the most recognizable paintings in the history of art, 'Starry Night' was painted from the asylum at Saint-Rémy-de-Provence, where van Gogh voluntarily admitted himself after mutilating his own ear. The painting is an idealized view, with an invented village and omission of the iron bars on his window. Art historian Sven Loevgren describes 'Starry Night' as "an infinitely expressive picture which symbolizes the final absorption of the artist by the cosmos". **641 dots**

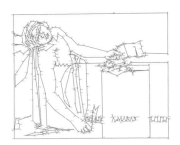

Page 30

The Death of Marat, 1793 by Jacques-Louis David
(1748–1825)

Jean-Paul Marat was an outspoken journalist in the French Revolution, murdered by 24-year-old Charlotte Corday who blamed Marat for the escalating violence of the Revolution. David was asked by the revolutionary government to glorify Marat as a martyr. His depiction of Marat in an almost hypnotic position in the bath, devoid of physical imperfections, is considered an intentional work of propaganda. **487 dots**

Page 31

The Arnolfini Portrait, 1434 by Jan van Eyck
(1390–1441)

Contrary to popular belief, this portrait painting of Giovanni di Nicolao Arnolfini and his wife does not depict their wedding. Nor is his wife pregnant, but rather she is holding up her dress in the contemporary fashion. The ornate Latin signature above the mirror translates as 'Jan van Eyck was here 1434'. Van Eyck often inscribed his pictures in a witty manner. **627 dots**

Page 32

The Kiss, 1909 by Gustav Klimt
(1862–1918)

The embracing couple of 'The Kiss' are entwined in elaborate robes influenced by both the earlier Arts and Craft movement and the contemporary Art Nouveau style. The painting is composed of oil paint with applied layers of gold leaf, giving a sparkling appearance. Klimt's career was on the downside before he produced this work, but before the painting had even been finished it was bought for a then-record 25,000 crowns, and today it is considered invaluable. **585 dots**

Page 33

The Laughing Cavalier, 1624 by Frans Hals (1580–1666)

The most notable fact about 'The Laughing Cavalier' other than the rich costume is that the subject is not actually laughing, but rather smiling in a knowing way, amplified by his upturned moustache. He is also not a cavalier, but perhaps a man soon to be betrothed (the painting's title was granted in the Victorian Times to convey his swagger and vitality). **463 dots**

Page 34

A Bar at the Folies-Bergère, 1882 by Édouard Manet (1832–1883)

Numerous articles have been written simply about the perspectives of the scene shown in the mirror of this famous work. The Folies-Bergère was a nightclub in Paris famed for its prostitutes, so is the barmaid more than a barmaid? And is the man in the reflection talking to her even though the angles look different? This painting was Impressionist pioneer Manet's last major work. **853 dots**

Page 35

Vase with 12 Sunflowers, 1888 by Vincent van Gogh (1853–1890)

Van Gogh created two series of still life paintings based on sunflowers, a first one in 1887 showing them lying on the ground and a second one of sunflowers in a vase. He painted the series in anticipation of the arrival in Arles of his friend Paul Gauguin, as a decoration for the studio they would share. **593 dots**

Page 36

The Clothed Maja, c. 1800 by Francisco de Goya (1746–1828)

De Goya painted 'The Naked Maja' at the end of the 18th century, depicting a beautiful, reclining woman. A few years later he painted the exact same scene – but with clothes on his subject. The painting was originally owned by the Spanish Prime Minister, Manuel de Godoy, who had a reputation for womanizing. It is reported that he hung the clothed version of the painting in front of the naked version in his room, so the latter could be revealed at any time. **604 dots**